Mind Hacking Secrets

How to Overcome Self-sabotaging Thinking, Master Your Focus and Live a Successful and Positive Life on Your Own Terms

Jay Laurson

© Copyright 2020 - All rights reserved.

The content contained within this book may not be reproduced, duplicated or transmitted without direct written permission from the author or the publisher.

Under no circumstances will any blame or legal responsibility be held against the publisher, or author, for any damages, reparation, or monetary loss due to the information contained within this book, either directly or indirectly.

Legal Notice:

This book is copyright protected. It is only for personal use. You cannot amend, distribute, sell, use, quote or paraphrase any part, or the content within this book, without the consent of the author or publisher.

Disclaimer Notice:

Please note the information contained within this document is for educational and entertainment purposes only. All effort has been executed to present accurate, up to date, reliable, complete information. No warranties of any kind are declared or implied. Readers acknowledge that the author is not engaging in the rendering of legal, financial, medical or professional advice. The content within this book has been derived from various sources.

Please consult a licensed professional before attempting any techniques outlined in this book.

By reading this document, the reader agrees that under no circumstances is the author responsible for any losses, direct or indirect, that are incurred as a result of the use of information contained within this document, including, but not limited to, errors, omissions, or inaccuracies.

Table of Contents

INTRODUCTION 1

CHAPTER 1: OUR SABOTAGING WAYS 6
    THE DEVIL IS IN THE NEGATIVITY 9
    OUR ANXIOUS MINDS 15

CHAPTER 2: THE WEAPONS OF SELF-SABOTAGE 19
    IMPOSTER SYNDROME 20
    SPLITTING 22
    THE MIND READER 24
    OVER-GENERALIZING 26
    THE NEGATIVE BIAS 27
    UNREALISTIC EXPECTATIONS 28
    PEOPLE PLEASING 30
    TARDINESS 32

CHAPTER 3: ARE OUR WIRES CROSSED? 34
    SET WAYS OF SABOTAGE 35
    REWIRING OUR BRAINS 38

CHAPTER 4: WEAPONS AGAINST SELF-SABOTAGING 46
    CHALLENGE YOUR NEGATIVE THOUGHTS 46
    SHOE ON THE OTHER FOOT 48
    RELINQUISH CONTROL OF THINGS OUT OF YOUR REACH 49
    COUNTERACT THE NEGATIVE BIAS 51
    MINIMIZE YOUR EXPECTATIONS 52
    SET SOLID GOALS AND PLANS 53
    PRACTICE MAKES PERFECT 55

CHAPTER 5: A HEALTHIER LIFESTYLE FOR A HEALTHIER MIND 57
    WHAT IS MINDFULNESS? 58
    HOW TO BE MORE MINDFUL 61
    MENTAL HEALTH AND A HEALTHY DIET 63
    WAYS IN WHICH HEALTHY EATING IMPROVES MENTAL HEALTH 64
    A DIET FOR BETTER MENTAL HEALTH 66
    MENTAL HEALTH AND EXERCISE 66
    WHAT EXERCISE IS GOOD FOR THE BRAIN? 67

CHAPTER 6: WHAT IS SUCCESS ANYWAY? 69

FAILURE, FRIEND OR FOE? 71
CONCLUSION 74
REFERENCES 77

Introduction

Life can feel like a never-ending race. We're all rushing around trying to fit everything into the limited amount of time we have here. Some of us know exactly what we want, but don't know how to get it. We feel stuck or limited by our environment or opportunities. Others have no clue what they want, and therefore have no idea what they are doing or how to get anywhere. They feel completely lost.

Then, there are also people out there who, much to everyone else's annoyance, seem to know exactly what they want, and they also seem to know exactly how to get it. We sit there and watch them sprinting ahead of us, and this only discourages us more by making us feel like failures in our own lives. We wonder what they know that we don't know, and we become resentful and unhappy. It's difficult not to let it affect us because we can't help but take it personally. However, we shouldn't take it personally - and we definitely shouldn't let it affect us.

What we don't always realize is that everyone is trying to figure it out as they go, just like we are. It's very likely that, although it may not look like it, they too feel lost or unsure of what they are doing at times. Everyone's journey and process are different, and we don't know what stage they are at in their lives. We are all trying to be the best versions of ourselves we can possibly be. We all want to be successful and happy, and we want to feel like we've made our mark on this world. We develop dreams and set goals for ourselves so that we can work towards achieving them.

We also all experience setbacks, failures and struggles.

Whoever you are, and whichever category you fall into, things aren't always how we perceive them to be. The reality is that we never know what is going on in someone else's life. Everybody has struggled to stay motivated, focused and positive in the face of all the obstacles that push them to fail. Even the most successful people out there have gone through rough times, and we don't know what they had to overcome to get to where they are. We're all on this Earth together, and it's important to know that you are not alone, that your struggles are not greater than anyone else's, and neither are your successes less than anyone else's.

It took me realizing this to come to the conclusion that my own lack of success was nobody else's fault but my own. I had to face the fact that I was the one holding myself back by not focusing on improving myself, and by not focusing on getting what I wanted out of life. I was becoming side-tracked by what other people were doing, and I was losing sight of what I was meant to be doing. You may not want to admit it to yourself, but most of the time you are your own worst enemy.

It's so easy to blame everyone but yourself for why your life hasn't turned out the way you wanted it to or thought it would.

It's something I used to do all the time. I used to look at everyone else around me, and think they seemed so much better off than I am, so much happier and more successful. I wondered what they had that I didn't, and how they were able to get everything they wanted when I couldn't. It can be easier to feel this way or to shift the blame for why you aren't successful onto others instead of yourself, but that won't really help you in any tangible way. When you stop blaming others and start looking at yourself with more honesty, you can start making positive changes in your life that will help you become a better version of yourself and will help you to continue to grow and become stronger and more resilient to life's adversities. Only then will you begin to make the progress necessary to achieve all the things you want out of life.

Perhaps there are people out there who are more successful than you are, but that isn't really the point. The point is that we shouldn't be worrying about why or how they got there when you haven't. You should rather be focusing your energy on learning how you can get there. When I realized this, I felt as though my life had been turned upside down. It unlocked something in me that motivated me to learn more. I became obsessed with trying to figure out how I could change myself in a positive way that would help me get the things I wanted out of my life.

This is how I began my journey into self-discovery, how I began to learn about how I could change my thinking and train my own brain to do what I wanted, rather than continue to stand by powerless as my brain controlled and sabotaged me. It was through this journey that the creation of this book began. This book aims to set you on your own path of self-discovery. It offers the building blocks of knowledge that will help you begin to understand yourself and the way your mind works. It teaches you the importance of introspection and having an understanding of how your brain works. It shows you the ways in which your unconscious mind leads you to engage in self-sabotaging thinking, and how this leads to self-sabotaging behaviors that stop you from being happy and successful. It explains the inner workings of your mind, and how this causes you to think and act in self-sabotaging ways without even realizing it.

One of the greatest obstacles we face in trying to gain success is mastering focus and control over our own minds. Sometimes it can feel like we have absolutely no control over our thinking at all. In fact, it can feel like our brains are actively working against us, holding us back and putting us down, and, to make matters worse, you are powerless to stop it. It also highlights the kinds of self-sabotaging thoughts you may fall victim to.

The good news is that you aren't powerless. There are skills and tools that can be learned to help you gain the control and focus you need. After teaching you to recognize your self-sabotaging thoughts and behaviors, this book will teach you how to combat them by training your brain to counteract the sabotaging thoughts that influence your behavior. It highlights better, more positive ways of thinking and behaving that will help you change your mindset and your life. You will learn about how to rewire your brain using a deeper understanding of your conscious mind and techniques from cognitive behavioral therapy Then, it will introduce you to mindfulness and explain how this can help you manage and regulate your emotions and sharpen your focus. It also shows you the benefits of living a healthier lifestyle, through a healthy diet and exercise, to better improve your brain's functioning.

You will begin to raise important questions about what you want to achieve in your life by wondering what success is and how it can mean different things to different people. We will discuss our relationship with failure and question whether fear is really a bad thing that should be avoided in our lives, or if it is a necessary part of life that helps us shape our goals and teaches us about ourselves and the world around us. By the end of the book, you will have the knowledge, skills, and tools to be able to take back control of your thoughts, train your brain and gain back your focus. By doing this, you can take the necessary steps to live a happy and successful life on your own terms.

Chapter 1: Our Sabotaging Ways

The first thing you need to accept is that self-sabotage is more common in your life than you may even realize. In the race of life, most of us are running with blinders on. We don't stop and take the time to think about what we're actually doing in the present moment. We don't take inventory of our mental and physical states, we don't always question if we are doing the right thing, and we also don't recognize the ways in which we could be harming ourselves. If you do stop and take note, you may begin to see that you have unhealthy relationships, whether they are in your personal life or professional life, that you're stuck in a rut and you aren't achieving any of your goals, or that you keep finding yourself repeating the same mistakes.

This is the evidence you need to find out that you have been self-sabotaging yourself. It starts with self-sabotaging thoughts which lead to sabotaging behaviors, such as procrastination, avoidance, and causing unnecessary conflict in your life. In order to learn how to stop these harmful thoughts and behaviors, you first need to gain a better understanding of the complexity of your mind. Your brain is an amazing organ, capable of achieving much more than you allow it to. Without an understanding of how it works, you are missing vital pieces of information that could help you learn how to control your thinking and your behavior.

Your mind is made up of consciousness and unconsciousness, and these two parts are very intimately connected in ways that psychologists are still working to understand. Thanks to the work and research of Sigmund Freud, we now realize the importance of the unconscious mind, and we recognize the effects and influence it can have on our lived experience. Through Freud's research, we have learned that the unconscious domain is not always the most rational part of our mind and that our impulses and unconscious thoughts can be somewhat of a mystery to us. Luckily, there is more to us than just this. We also have a stream of consciousness that makes up the more rational, coherent side of our thinking. We make sense of the world around us and understand it through these thoughts.

Problems begin to pop up when these two parts of our mind find themselves at war with one another. Our more rational side tries to suppress the unconscious, and the unconscious tries to break through this suppression and make itself heard. Sometimes, the unconscious mind manages to sneak through these barriers in little - and often unexpected - ways. It can be through our dreams or through us acting out unpredictably, like when you lose your temper at someone who doesn't deserve it. You can't talk to the person who you really have a problem with, because you're trying to avoid having a fight with them. Maybe because you don't know how to talk to them about it, or maybe it's your boss and you're afraid of jeopardizing your job. Instead, you pick someone else to lose your temper at. Someone less intimidating or less likely to retaliate. The poor soul bears the brunt of it because you're suppressing your feelings and thoughts, and your unconscious mind can't hold on to that anger for long.

Thus, it forces it out the first chance it gets.

When we're dealing with something unsettling or something we aren't quite ready to look at emotionally, we tend to bury it in our unconscious mind to hide it away. It could be things you don't want to admit to yourself, that remind you of past traumas, or that make you feel horrible about yourself. The reasoning behind it doesn't really matter. What does matter is that this is not a healthy or effective way of dealing with things. By choosing to ignore certain things we are feeling or thinking, and by keeping a closed lid on our unconscious mind, we are locking a part of ourselves away. It also puts us at a massive disadvantage. Eventually, everything will come out and it will come out in ways you have no control over. Ways that can have a negative impact on your happiness and success, especially when the consequence of this is that you end up sabotaging yourself.

On the other hand, if we fight this impulse to turn a blind eye to our unconscious mind, and instead stop and take the time to unpack the feelings and thoughts that live there, we can learn a lot about ourselves. We can begin to understand ourselves better, gain knowledge about why we think the way we do and how our thoughts - unconscious or conscious - can have an impact on our behavior. Having this kind of knowledge about yourself will help you change and control your own thoughts and behavior better. You will be able to get to the root of what is causing you to sabotage yourself, and you can influence your behavior in more positive ways that help you achieve success rather than hinder it. It's quite similar to the movie, Inception, except the aim is to be awake while you're delving into your subconscious. The next step is knowing what to look for once you've successfully incepted your mind. To do this, you will need to understand what causes sabotaging thoughts.

The Devil Is in the Negativity

One of the biggest contributors to self-sabotaging thoughts is negativity. It is the fuel that drives self-sabotage and stops us from reaching our full potential. It pollutes our minds with toxic thoughts that distort reality and cloud our judgment. Self-doubt, harsh self-criticisms, and self-chastising thoughts are examples of the kinds of negative thinking we're talking about. It makes us feel anxious, keeps us in our comfort zone, and stops us from taking risks and going for what we want in life.

You could think that you aren't smart enough to go to university so you don't bother to apply and your dreams of becoming a lawyer go out the window. You could be overly critical of yourself, criticizing every little detail of your appearance while you get ready to leave the house, shattering your confidence. You could be way too hard on yourself, picking apart your failures and mistakes rather than picking yourself up and learning from them. All those times you berated yourself or thought you were a failure every time you made a mistake, you were losing yourself in unnecessary negative thoughts. This negative part of your mind tells you: you aren't good enough, you should just give up; and when you listen to and believe these thoughts, it squishes your confidence. It becomes harmful to your self-esteem and your sense of self-worth. This can lead to depression, anger, and resentment towards yourself and the world. It affects your behavior and causes you to act in self-sabotaging ways that stop you from progressing in life as you should.

A lot of our negative thoughts come from our constant need to compare ourselves to those around us. It's difficult not to compare ourselves to others. No matter how many times you try to block everything out and just focus on your own life and success, you can't help but look around you and wonder how everyone else is doing. You try to gauge if they are doing better or worse than you financially, professionally, and even in their interpersonal lives. Whether it's your former school friends, colleagues, neighbors or family members, you seem to always compare yourself to them and measure your success against theirs. We've all met that person who seems to be doing so much better than us. They seem so much happier, more successful, they have more money, and everyone seems to like them more. This, in turn, makes you feel bad about your life and accomplishments. Suddenly, you start to see yourself in a negative light. You feel like a failure and you start beating yourself up. You ask yourself why you haven't achieved as much as they have, and you start to wonder what they have that you don't and where you are going wrong.

I had a friend who fell victim to constant comparisons to those around her, and it left her in a puddle of misery. Catherine found herself comparing her life to her friends' lives when she got back from traveling abroad for two years after university. She was one of those free spirits who loved to travel, and she put all of her resources and focus into jetting off to wherever her heart desired. However, not many people choose the path that she chose. In fact, the vast majority of people stay at home after university and get stable jobs to work towards their careers, financial stability, and independence.

When Catherine finally came home she realized this for herself. She was forced to stop and take inventory of her life. When she saw how all of her friends had progressed, she couldn't help but notice her lack of progression. She realized that the life she had been living for the past two years looked very different from those around her. Negative thoughts began to cloud her mind. Had she made the wrong choices that lead her down the wrong path? She began to feel as though she hadn't achieved as much as her friends.

Her closest friend from school, Mary, seemed so much more successful than her. Mary was engaged and settled down in an apartment that she and her fiancé had just bought. She seemed happy and independent, living an all-around stable life. In comparison, Catherine didn't have a penny to her name. She didn't have a place of her own and she had to move back in with her parents when she got back from her travels. She hadn't even thought about marriage for the past two years; never being anywhere long enough to form a lasting connection with anyone. Her job prospects were not great since all of her work experience consisted of odd jobs she had picked up here and there on her travels. She became very unsettled by this revelation and it caused her to feel very dissatisfied with herself and her life.

Truthfully, she felt left behind, like she had made the wrong choices that had now set her back two years. She felt frantic and pressured to try and catch up with her friends, which in turn overwhelmed her and left her not knowing where to begin. This began a very toxic and depressive spiral that just fed itself in her mind until she barely even wanted to leave her house. Catherine's mind became clouded by negativity caused by her allowing herself to compare her life and her journey with her friends. She allowed this negativity to take over her autonomy, and she became a prisoner trapped in her own mind. She forgot that she had her own journey and that what she wanted out of her life was not the same as Mary did. She never wanted the life that Mary had, but she lost her focus. She could no longer see that, and she ended up sabotaging herself - and this lead to her not achieving her success.

I'm sure we can all sympathize with Catherine. After all, we've all been there, trapped in our own minds and plagued by negativity due to comparing ourselves and our accomplishments to people with very different goals and dreams than your own. However, have you ever wondered why exactly we fall victim to this self-destructive thinking?

From a very young age, we learn from mirroring others. You must have seen this in action many times when around children. Maybe you're playing with your nieces or nephews and you pull a funny face, and they copy you by pulling the same face back. In fact, this happened to me not so long ago. I was having dinner at a friend's house one night and her one-and-a-half-year-old little girl was sitting next to me at the dinner table. She was very interested in me since I was a new and exciting face in her home. She was watching me very closely and became fascinated at what I was doing at the dinner table; how I sat, how I held my cutlery, how I ate my food. At one point, I reached over to pour myself a glass of water. I put the jug down, reached for my glass and took a nice refreshing sip. Not even five seconds after I put my glass down, she reached over and grabbed my glass off the table, almost spilling its contents before she managed to steady it. She then mirrored my actions by taking a sip of her own. This is known as social learning theory.

When we get older, this method of learning continues as we begin to form our identities and understand ourselves in relation to the world around us. Instead of learning how to drink water out of a glass or brush our teeth, we begin to learn about how to behave socially. Like that time one of your peers was completely unprepared for their speech in class and got a massive scolding from your teacher in front of the class, which left them completely humiliated, and it taught you to never repeat their mistake and always be prepared for your speeches. We also begin to shape our ideas about who we are and what we want to achieve during our lives. We develop role models, we think to ourselves, "That's who I want to be one day," and we begin to model ourselves after them in the hopes that we will one day achieve what they have. While this is a necessary process during our development, it also has an unhealthy side to it. Unfortunately, through this process, we also develop the terrible habit of comparing ourselves with those around us. We wonder why someone else is dating the person you like. Are they smarter than you? More attractive?

Unfortunately, as adults, we continue to do this, even though you are no longer a child or adolescent learning about the world. Surely, by now, you should know who you are and what you want out of life well enough to just focus on your own journey and work hard at making your goals a reality. Surely, this is all you need to be happy and successful without a care in the world. Sadly this is not the case. The very thing that helped shape you now becomes the enemy that works against you and actually stops you from achieving your goals. To make matters worse, this process of comparison is so deeply ingrained at this point that it has now become an unconscious process in our brains that can, if left unchecked, cause a lot of struggle and turmoil in our lives. When someone has something you don't have or they achieve something you want, you can't help but wonder why it wasn't you. Perhaps there's something wrong with you. We've all been in this position, perhaps someone else got a promotion at work over you, even though you feel you worked just as hard or that you are just as capable. You begin to take it personally, and you then begin to compare yourself to your colleague who got the promotion.

Our Anxious Minds...

Anxiety can also be a big contributing factor to having self-sabotaging thoughts and acting on self-sabotaging behavior. When we feel anxious, we begin to behave in avoidant ways, as we try to get away from the things and people that cause us anxiety. Anxiety seems to be such a useless emotion, and it begs the question of why we experience it in the first place. Especially if it causes so many unnecessary problems in our lives. However, although anxiety may be unpleasant to feel and it can have negative effects on us, it does serve a purpose in our lives. We feel anxious because it's our brain's way of protecting us from danger. It relates back to a process in the brain known as fight or flight. Before we developed our society and the technology that we have today, we had a lot more danger around us that we needed to be anxious about. The flight or fight response in our brains is a process that is meant to automatically protect us from perceived danger.

If a predator is lurking in the bushes waiting to pounce and we happen to notice it in time, then our brains will take over to ensure we get out of there as soon as possible. The best way to get away from danger is to run away and avoid it at all costs, and we need this alarm system in place in our brains to ensure that we do this. If we didn't have this process in our brains, then we would freeze and leave ourselves vulnerable to the danger we are faced with. We would also be a lot more reckless in our daily lives. If we didn't feel anxious standing on the roof of a tall building while we looked down at the ground below us, then we would be much more inclined to hang over the edge to see what happened. Anxiety also has a much more practical purpose in our daily lives today. It keeps us moving. The anxiety you feel to meet your deadlines at work or at university pushes you to finish your work on time. If we didn't feel this pressure and anxiety, we would most likely become indifferent and not get anything done at all.

Anxiety becomes problematic in our lives when we allow it to take over our lives. Anxiety is linked to feelings of being in danger, and when our brains begin to fear things that aren't really dangerous to us at all, it has the potential to cause an unhealthy pattern of response to that perceived danger. When you feel anxious about something, you will act in one of two ways. You can act in ways that allow you to avoid the perceived danger, and your brain will then breathe out a sigh of relief, thinking it has actively and successfully saved you from danger. It will then take this to mean that when it feels anxious, avoidance is the best course of action, and it will continue to prompt you to avoid things that trigger your anxiety. The default response to danger, whether it was real or not, has, in this case, become avoidance.

This is not a good way to deal with anxiety because it causes you to fear things that you don't really have to be afraid of. It also limits you and keeps you isolated from the world by preventing you from experiencing new things. The more things you avoid out of fear, the more afraid you will become, until, eventually, your entire life could become ruled by your fears and anxieties. Another way you could act in response to your anxiety would be to challenge it. You could face the things that cause you anxiety head-on. This is called exposure therapy, and when you do this, you are showing your brain that it has nothing to be afraid of. Remember, the danger your brain is telling you you're in is not always real, and when you expose yourself to the source of your anxiety and nothing bad happens, your brain will learn to stop fearing that thing. The more you challenge your anxieties, the less you will have to fear.

I had a colleague who was a very socially anxious person. He didn't like to be in situations that caused him anxiety, and as a means of coping with this, he avoided many social gatherings because his brain was telling him that by doing so he was protecting himself. He was afraid of going out of his comfort zone and of being vulnerable because this opened him up to being hurt or socially ridiculed and embarrassed. At first, his colleagues would make an effort with him, and they would invite him out in an attempt to bring him out of his shell and get to know him better. However, time and time again he would reject their offers, preferring to go home rather than put himself through the social anxiety he knew he would be faced with had he gone out with them.

One day, he woke up and realized that he had no friends and that he was very lonely and unhappy in the isolated life that he lived. He realized that by not putting in the effort and time with his colleagues socially, he was not putting himself out there enough, and he had no one to blame for his loneliness but himself. He slowly began to make an effort with those around him, and in so doing so, he was challenging his social anxiety. He began to overcome his fear of social situations, until he eventually worked his way up to going out with his colleagues. He began to realize that he didn't have anything to fear, and he began to feel a lot better. He realized that his colleagues were really nice people and he had a lot in common with. He began to wonder where the anxiety he once felt when thinking about socializing with them even came from in the first place.

Chapter 2: The Weapons of Self-sabotage

The next step in understanding how we sabotage ourselves is learning how to recognize some of the common self-sabotaging thoughts that manifest in our minds. By being able to recognize and then gain a better understanding of them and where they stem from, you will begin to be able to see how your thinking has become clouded and distorted. You can then begin to develop ways to overcome them by gaining a better perspective on things. The self-sabotaging thoughts will begin to crumble and fall apart the more you inspect and question them. Your self-sabotaging thoughts are like a virus that can't survive in the open air.

It is important to note that there are many self-sabotaging thoughts and that most of them hold some similarities to one another. This is because all of these thoughts come from the same place. They come from our negativity and our anxiety, which I will go into more detail on later in this book. For now, I have selected a few examples of self-sabotaging thoughts that will begin to highlight how to recognize them. Going through a comprehensive list of unhealthy thoughts is beyond the scope of this book. By understanding the ones I outline, you will begin to see a pattern in this thinking, and you will then be able to start developing the ability to identify more on your own.

Imposter Syndrome

Have you ever felt like your accomplishments were not your own? Like at any moment someone is going to turn around, look you in the eye and say, "Hey buster, I'm on to you." Then you were experiencing what is known as imposter syndrome, and you aren't alone in having these feelings. Some of the most successful and famous people in the world have admitted to feeling it, despite everything in their lives standing testament to those feelings not being valid at all. It happens because we all experience the world through our own subjective eyes. We exist in our minds and through our own little universe we see all of our shortcomings and embarrassments, whether we want to acknowledge them or not, they exist.

We don't have the same experience as others around us, because for the most part what we see of other people are polished, well thought out versions of them. The version of themselves that they allow the rest of the world to see. We don't see the same embarrassments and shortcomings we see in ourselves, and because of this, we automatically assume they don't have any. How does this relate to being successful you ask? Well, when we accomplish things we feel imposter syndrome because we get it in our heads that we're flawed and not as accomplished as other people who seem so much more put together than we are.

Imagine it's your dream to be an actor, and you've worked really hard to be one. You've spent countless hours reading scripts and in acting classes or performing in school plays. You idolize famous actors in movies, and you envision yourself in their place one day. Then, when you finally get your big break and you land that part you know will catapult your acting career, you begin to feel uneasy. You feel out of place on set as you rehearse your lines, and you feel like a sitting duck getting your makeup up done while you get into character. You don't see yourself as you would see any other actor you idealized who has sat in your place, because to you, you aren't anything special and they seem so much more accomplished than you are. However, it may come as a surprise to realize that it's more than likely countless other brilliant actors who you look up to have felt exactly the same in your place. Even if you don't see them, everybody has flaws and doubts about themselves. We're all human and we're all struggling to come to grips with ourselves and our accomplishments.

Splitting

Also known as black and white thinking, splitting is a rigid and binary way of looking at the world. Everything is either good or bad and you tend not to recognize or even understand anything in between these two extremes. This way of thinking oversimplifies your understanding of people and the world around you, and it can stop you from experiencing things fully. The world is a colorful place, with many nuances and unique occurrences and experiences. Having a richer, more full-bodied understanding of the world helps you get so much more out of everything. We tend to exercise splitting because the world can be very overwhelming and confusing. Simplifying it into binary terms is a way to make sense of it all. However, if that is the only way you are able to make sense of the world, you will begin to find that this kind of thinking will eventually affect your self-image, your relationships, and it will inevitably hold you back from achieving success.

Your self-image becomes affected because you end up being way too hard on yourself. You view yourself as either a good or a bad person. You limit your autonomy by doing this because you begin to hold yourself to impossibly high standards. If you do one bad thing you're a terrible human being. You could end up becoming a people pleaser, unable to say no to things even if they cause you to become inconvenienced. You become afraid to let anyone down. If you promised a friend to go for dinner, but on the planned night you feel exhausted and not up to going at all, you'll compromise yourself and go anyway because you don't want to let them down. You split what is happening into two categories, either you go and fulfill your promise, being the good friend that you are, or you cancel and let your friend down, which means you are then a bad friend and also a bad person. This is an unfair evaluation of the situation and it causes you unnecessary stress as you begin to try and live up to your own unrealistic expectations of yourself.

It also affects your relationships in a similar way, because you also tend to think in these binary terms about the people around you. Your colleagues, friends, and romantic partners are only as good as their good deeds. If they let you down in any way, they become bad people and are judged way too harshly based on one action. These kinds of relationships can become toxic and extremely tiring to maintain, and it puts a lot of unnecessary pressure and strain on your relationships. People have both good and bad traits, but we shouldn't judge people on their bad traits alone. After all, no one is perfect - and that includes you.

This kind of thinking also hinders your success because splitting causes you to unrealistically strive for perfection. Failure of any kind and in any form is simply unacceptable. If you fail in even the smallest way, then you are a failure. There's no room for mistakes or for learning from your mistakes and growing from them. This can lead to countless unfinished projects or abandoned pursuits as you decide to give up rather than carry on and try your best. If it's not perfect then it's not worth it.

The Mind Reader

We all do this quite a lot. We tend to think that we know what other people are thinking, or that we somehow know when someone is judging or criticizing us. We even go so far as to assume what their judgments or criticism are. To a certain extent, we all have the ability to gauge what other people are thinking through reading body language, facial expressions, reading social cues, and through interpreting the subtext in what people say. If we didn't have this ability we would all be stumbling around in the dark every time we tried to socialize with other people.

What we don't realize is that this ability is very limited, and it only ever really works out in your favor when used correctly in a conversation with others. Relying too much on assuming you know what others are thinking can lead to some really embarrassing and awkward misunderstandings in social situations. It can also lead to you isolating yourself from people and not getting to know them because of your misconceptions about them. It's also a sign that you care too much about what other people think about you, which in itself is quite an unhealthy way of living your life.

Truthfully, whatever is going on in someone else's head is none of our business; their thoughts belong to them alone and concerning yourself with it is a waste of your time. In all likelihood, they probably very rarely think about you, since most people are too preoccupied with thinking about themselves, or what others might be thinking about them, to even consider you in any real detail. Even if they are judging and criticizing you, it's not your problem until they make it your problem by voicing their thoughts out loud to you. Until that happens, try not to let what others may or may not be thinking concern you. This may seem to be easier said than done, but in the long run, you will feel quite liberated with the freedom this gives you.

It's also worth knowing that the judgments and criticisms you perceive others to have of you are more a reflection of how you are judging yourself than any real representation of what they are thinking. They are reflections of your own insecurities that you are mirroring in the perceived thoughts of those around you. Consider meeting someone for the first time. Say it's a friend of a friend, and you're insecure about their friendship because you self-consciously feel like their friendship takes away from your own. In your interaction with this new person, you begin to view everything they do and say with these feelings clouding your judgment of the situation. You feel like they are talking too much, or that they are trying to take your friend's attention away from you. You assume they don't like you and that they are trying to sabotage your relationship with your friend. In actual fact, you're assuming you know what this person is thinking, and you are highlighting your own insecurities in their actions. You are the one doing the sabotaging in these situations, and you're stopping yourself from potentially making a new friend.

Over-generalizing

If you've ever avoided certain people, situations, or places based on one bad previous experience you've had in relation to them, then you probably have the tendency to overgeneralize things. One awkward social interaction with someone tells you that they're awkward and should be avoided to prevent any further awkward social interactions, or one bad experience at a restaurant means that every experience there will obviously be bad as well. This way of thinking limits you from doing and experiencing a lot of things because it causes you to put unnecessary restrictions in place. You begin to make snap judgments of what you do and don't like too quickly, without really giving yourself the time to be won over by things.

This happened to me once when I tried to introduce a friend to live blues music. He loved to go and watch live music, and I thought he would love this little blues bar I enjoyed going to on some nights when I wanted a good night out. However, he didn't share my enthusiasm since he had a bad experience going out with me once when I insisted that he join me in trying out a live music event that I had no one else to accompany me to. He ended up coming with and it turned out to be an awful night; the music was terrible, the venue was too crowded, and we had an all-around terrible time.

Nevertheless, I was determined to make up for that experience, and I just knew this blues bar would be right up his alley. After much resistance and grumbling along the way, I managed to get him to go out with me one night, but I may as well not have even bothered. He had already decided that he wasn't going to have a good night and nothing that happened that night was going to change that. He can be quite stubborn and his stubbornness held firm as he judged the night based on his past experience going out with me that one time. He wasn't impressed with the venue, they didn't serve his preferred beer, and the music was mediocre at best. To this day he even insists that he doesn't like live blues music at all. I have long since stopped bothering to try and change his mind.

The Negative Bias

Research shows that out of all the experiences you have in a day, negative, positive, and neutral, you will pick at and focus on the negatives the most. We will skip over all the good things that happened to us that day and fill our thoughts and feelings with the bad. This is known as negative bias. Our brains do this because we tend to learn more from the negative things that happen to us, rather than the positive ones. We learn more about how to behave through what we ought not to do rather than what we ought to do. Those times when you were told off by your mom for being rude to your grandfather by not giving him a hug stood out more than all the times your mother praised you for doing the right thing.

We also tend to use a negative bias in relation to our accomplishments. When we achieve something great, instead of enjoying our success and allowing ourselves to feel good about ourselves, we tend to look for the things we did wrong or could have improved on. We criticize ourselves and try to pick out the errors. If you ever stop to really think about how you do this, you may come to the realization that this is an absolutely absurd way to respond to the good things that happen to you. If you're never able to enjoy your success and praise yourself for your accomplishments, then what are you working so hard for? You're chasing something you don't even know how to get. You will never be satisfied with what you achieve in your life because nothing will ever be good enough for you. You will always put yourself down, no matter how far up the success ladder you manage to climb. You'll reach every new stage in your life, stop and criticize yourself, wonder what's next, and continue climbing.

Unrealistic Expectations

When we are younger, we have a tendency to think that what is going on in our heads has a direct impact on what is happening in the real world. We think that just because we think something, or want something, that it exists in the real world or we will get it without having to do much about it. A child might go to bed and wish for a horse to appear in the garden the next day to play with, and be confused about why there isn't a horse waiting there in the morning. This is also called magical thinking, and although we are meant to outgrow this, this kind of thinking sometimes follows us into adulthood.

Superstitious thinking is an example of this. We could think that a bad hair day is a sign of a bad day, and so we go about our day waiting for all the bad things to come our way. The phenomenon known as the placebo effect is another example of how adults practice magical thinking. However, magical thinking can also cause you to self-sabotage because it can lead to you creating unrealistic expectations for things in your head. Expectations of ourselves, of others, and of future events and situations. We then have a tendency to pin our happiness on the eventual fulfillment of these expectations. This can be a dangerous game to play because, in reality, those expectations are not based on anything real and tangible. They are based on our hopes, desires, and ideas about things and situations in our environment. If those expectations are not met, which is quite likely, since things rarely pan out the way we want them to, then our happiness plummets. Since we pin our happiness on future events that we have no way of controlling, there is nothing we can do but feel let down when they don't go the way we had hoped.

Imagine you get it in your head that you're going to get a promotion at work, and you start to think how great your life will be once you get that promotion. You start to make plans for what you're going to do with the extra money you get from the pay rise. Maybe you can finally buy that new car you've been eyeing. This is going to be great! You're finally going to get the recognition you've been wanting at work and everyone is going to be so impressed by your new job title. Before you know it, your expectations have gotten out of hand, and your happiness has become dependent on it. Now imagine, you get passed over for someone else, and your colleague ends up getting the promotion instead of you. Your promotion. How would that make you feel? It may come as a shock, and it will definitely be difficult for you to accept or bounce back from.

When we fill our heads with unrealistic expectations, we are living in possibilities and future events that may never happen. We are not living in the moment and enjoying what the very real world around us has to offer. Life has many twists and turns; circumstances change, we change, and so should our goals - and actions aimed to achieve those goals. By allowing ourselves to have unrealistic expectations, we are also losing our ability to be adaptable and to be resilient to setbacks that stop us from reaching our goals. We are also letting ourselves off the hook for having to do the hard work necessary to get there.

People Pleasing

If you have a tendency to always say yes to things, even when it's to your detriment, and you struggle to use the word "no", as if it doesn't even exist in your vocabulary, then you are more than likely a people pleaser. Saying yes is so much easier than dealing with the consequences of saying no. After all, you want people to like you, and you don't want to let them down and give them a reason to not want to be friends with you anymore. This is also a means of avoiding conflict. Rather than standing your ground and deciding what you are and are not willing to do, you are choosing to just go along with what they want. The need to please others in this way comes from a low sense of self-worth. You don't respect yourself enough to set boundaries in place in your relationship, and because of this, people will most likely not respect you either.

We need boundaries because they speak to the world about how we would like to be treated, and they allow you to put in place a set of rules that builds up yourself self-worth. If you don't set these boundaries in place, then people will end up walking all over you and your relationships will end up suffering because of it. Your constant people-pleasing will also land you in some tricky situations. You may find yourself overtaxing your time and compromising your plans for someone else's, or you may find yourself double booking through promising multiple people a piece of your time that you don't have to give. You will inevitably end up letting people down anyway, and they will come to think of you as unreliable. On the other hand, you will form much stronger and longer-lasting bonds with people when your relationship with them is based on a foundation of respect. So, know your worth, and learn to respect yourself so that you can teach people how to respect you.

Tardiness

We all have that one friend who is constantly late to you everything you invite them to. At first, you put up with it because you like them and having them as a friend far outweighs the fact that they are a bit unreliable. When you make plans with them, you even tell them to be there half an hour to an hour early, so that you don't end up waiting around for them for too long. This can become tiresome and it can be frustrating, to say the least. Eventually, it leaves a sour taste in your mouth as you begin to think that your tardy friend thinks that their time is more valuable than yours. However, it might be worth knowing that always being late for things is actually another form of self-sabotaging behavior. The reason they are late may not be because, as they would like you to believe, they have poor time management or it's just a quirk in their personalities. It's a way for them to cope with anxiety and stress in their daily lives. It could be because of social anxiety, and because of this, they procrastinate getting ready and lose track of time. It can also be a way of shooting themselves in the foot.

Perhaps they are headed to a job interview and their fear of not getting the job causes them to self-sabotage by being late. That way, when they don't get the job, it wasn't their fault. It wasn't due to them being inadequate or unqualified in some way, and it definitely wasn't because they are a failure. It was due to them being late because of whatever excuse they use to cover up for their lateness. There's always an excuse for their tardiness, and it always completely lets them off the hook. Something like, "My car broke down." or "I couldn't find the place on my maps, with the address you sent me, I ended up driving around in circles." This form of self-sabotage may be neatly disguised, but it can stop you from achieving a lot in your life. It will stop you from ever really putting yourself out there and going for what you want. As much as you try to deny it and tell yourself that the reason you aren't succeeding isn't your fault, the only person you are fooling is yourself.

Chapter 3: Are Our Wires Crossed?

To fully understand how our negative and anxiety-riddled brains lead to self-sabotaging thoughts and behaviors without us even realizing it, we need to have a better understanding of the science behind how our brains work. Activity happens in the brain through neurons firing along axons that connect the neurons in your brain. This is how communication happens in your brain, and it's what creates your thinking and your actions. This entire process creates what are called neurological pathways. The more we act out a particular behavior, the more axons and dendrites form in association with that action. This causes a stronger link between the neurons associated with that behavior, and it allows for communication between these neurons to fire faster and father, reinforcing them and making them stronger. The stronger the connection, the more well known and used that neural pathway becomes in your brain. This is how habits are formed, they become automatic behaviors we act on without much thought or effort on our part.

Think of hiking. When you head off into the wilderness, you know where to go because of previous hikers who have used the same trail over and over again. Neurological pathways in the brain are like a well-used hiking trail that clearly marks the way. Your brain will begin to use the well-used neurological pathways by default, without you even noticing. This is why when you learn something new, at first it can seem so unnatural and difficult to grasp. You need to slow everything down so that you can learn it one step at a time and only after grasping how to do everything and spending a considerable amount of time practicing do you begin to gain confidence and feel like you are finally getting the hang of it. Learning how to drive a car is a very good example of this. Flash forward to a year after getting your driver's license and you can't even remember a time you weren't driving as you fly down the street with the radio blaring. Once those new neurological pathways related to driving have been established and you gain enough experience driving, they become reinforced and automatic. You no longer even have to think about all the different things you have to do in order to drive, you just do it.

In many ways, this is a good and necessary process to exist in the brain, since it helps us to learn and retain the skills we need to complete tasks and functions necessary for carrying out those tasks daily. However, it can also be used to create and reinforce bad pathways in the brain that cause bad habits and patterns of behavior that can cause you to continuously sabotage your own life without you even noticing.

Set Ways of Sabotage

When we repeat self-sabotaging thoughts and behaviors throughout our daily lives, we are forming and reinforcing bad neurological pathways in our brains. These become the normal default behaviors that we carry out every day because our brains don't know any better way of behaving. These thoughts and behaviors are unconscious and automatic, as we carry them out without even realizing or questioning them. Since we aren't even aware that they are happening, we are powerless to do anything to put a stop to them. We just fall into the same habits and patterns daily, creating a rigid pattern of thinking and behaving, allowing this to sabotage us and stop us from working towards achieving our goals and happiness. We are left at the mercy of our own brains.

Flashing back to my university days, I remember a classmate named Sasha who fell into one of these patterns of self-sabotage. She had a very unproductive way of getting on with her coursework. She would become very overwhelmed by the amount of work she had to do, which would cause her quite a bit of anxiety. To make matters worse, she didn't really enjoy the degree she was in, and this caused her to have quite negative thoughts about the course and the university that went a long way to demotivate her. All of this resulted in her avoiding her course work, she wasn't really interested in what she was learning and she tended to spend a lot of the time she should have been working on her assignments on procrastinating. Her work would pile up and as her deadlines got closer and closer, she would become increasingly more anxious and stressed out about getting her work done. This leads to more avoidance and procrastination until the absolute last minute, when she would pull all-nighters trying to finish all her work and meet her deadlines.

Despite her demotivation and her negative opinions about the university, she had no desire to fail and waste the time and money she had already put into her education. This resulted in her feeling pretty burned out from the whole ordeal, but somehow she always managed to reach her deadlines on time and after she handed in her assignments she would turn to me and say, "never again…" She would make all the promises to be better prepared next time and to work on her time management so that she didn't leave everything to the last minute again and cause herself so much unnecessary stress. However, these promises were never kept - every time she would find herself in the same cycle, allowing herself to procrastinate until the last minute time and time again. Her avoidance and procrastination towards her university work became her default behavior, and as such created a rigid pattern of self-sabotaging thoughts and behaviors in her brain that burnt her out. It also put her university degree at risk, and she never did perform to her full potential because she never gave herself the chance to do her work properly.

Sasha's behavior is only one example of how we sabotage ourselves, but there are countless others. The self-sabotaging thoughts mentioned in chapter 2 present themselves differently for everyone experiencing them, depending on their situations and goals. We are hard on ourselves, feed our self-doubt, and we allow this to paralyze us. This makes us afraid to put ourselves out there, and it stops us from reaching our full potential and achieving success. However, what they all have in common is that when we don't stop these patterns of sabotage, we are doing nothing to help ourselves achieve happiness and success. We are allowing our negativity and anxiety to affect our thinking in self-sabotaging ways that influence our behavior and reinforce the neurological pathways that connect them until they become automatic in our lives.

Rewiring Our Brains

Imagine what would happen if instead of allowing this to continue, we started to believe in ourselves. To focus more on the positive rather than the negative, and to start to recognize our successes and give ourselves credit where credit is due. Instead of looking at our mistakes or failures and letting them defeat us, we take them as learning curves that make us better equipped for future success. Be more positive, is that really the answer? Well, no… it's not really that simple or easy, because as much as people would like you to believe, turning off your negative thoughts is not as easy as flipping a switch and having them disappear. Most people would tell you to, "Keep your chin up!", or they would optimistically sing, "When life gives you lemons…" and think that they have done their part in helping you overcome your struggles. Unfortunately, life is more complicated than that.

We tend to look down on negativity, and we try to bury it by promoting positivity like it's your only saving grace in this world. This is because we believe that it is, that it's our only way to combat our negative thoughts. However, no matter how much we try and how hard we work at being positive, negativity is just a natural process that exists in our thinking, and it's impossible to stay positive all of the time. Sometimes we just have bad days and we want to yell and kick and scream at everything and everyone. Nothing is going right and no amount of positivity is going to change that.

Of course, I'm not trying to say that positivity isn't a good trait to have, and indeed, it has been proven that positivity can go a long way to help you achieve success. However, it's problematic to try to stay positive all of the time. Constant positivity doesn't really solve all of your problems. Sometimes trying to remain positive is a means of keeping that lid tightly locked on your unconscious mind. It allows you to sweep your problems under a nice, colorful positivity rug. You don't have to deal with the mess because you're just tucking it away out of sight. This is not a healthy way of dealing with things. If you don't tidy up under the rug and get rid of your mess once and for all, you're bound to find those problems pop up time and time again.

Even when you are in the best place you've ever been, emotionally, physically, and professionally, if you don't make an effort to understand yourself and where your negative thoughts and anxieties come from, you will never truly be safe from them. Besides, a little bit of negativity is good for you, it keeps you level-headed and it keeps things in perspective. The world isn't all good, and you need to recognize the bad in the world in order to prepare yourself for it. It's just as important to know that you can't let your life become ruled by negative thinking. We have to keep an eye on those negative thoughts because, if left unchecked, they could get completely out of hand. The problem with negativity is that it feeds itself, it builds and builds on itself until eventually you are completely overcome with it. One minute you're in a really good place in your life, things are going really well. You've set yourself achievable goals, and you're on the right path towards achieving them. You feel confident because you're finally getting somewhere, and success seems to be just around the corner.

Then, out of nowhere, something happens that completely derails you. It could be something small, one negative comment directed your way that plants a seed of doubt, or one negative criticism you unjustly direct at yourself. Maybe you experience a small failure that you turn into something bigger than it is in your mind. Other times it could be something big, a promotion at work that puts you under pressure to prove you deserved it. It could be a life-altering tragic event that has you questioning everything. Whether it starts big or small, these situations happen to you and they are out of your control. They put you under pressure, or they make you feel stressed. This causes your defenses to weaken and creates a breeding ground for negativity. If you allow the negativity to take root in your mind, it will completely take over. Before you realize it, the self-sabotaging begins.

This is what happened to a friend of mine, Sam, a very capable and successful salesman. Things were going well for him, almost too well. He had been working for the company for about two years when he was offered a promotion. Naturally, he was ecstatic to get some well-deserved recognition and a reward for all of his hard work and loyalty to the company. However, with the promotion came added responsibility, and he had a tendency to buckle under pressure. There was also a bit of backlash from colleagues who felt resentful that they themselves were not promoted. Sam started off confident, and he thought that he was ready for the challenge the promotion offered. He had worked hard to get to where he was, and he was ready to show his colleagues and superiors what he was capable of. He wanted to prove to them that they were right to promote him. Unfortunately, he didn't remain confident for long, as the pressure began to get to him, and he began to feel increasingly overwhelmed. The backlash from his colleagues didn't help either, and it planted a small seed of doubt in his mind.

That was all it took, his negativity towards himself grew, and it began to cloud his judgment. It stopped him from performing as well as he would have in his new role; he had lost focus on what he needed to do to be successful. He became anxious about going to work, and he procrastinated on doing his work. This made him feel like a failure. Every time he made a mistake, he would exaggerate and think it meant he was a failure. He felt like an imposter in the role. Like he hadn't really earned his position. He would overcompensate for shortcomings he thought other people thought he had. He began to think he knew what his colleagues or superiors were thinking and saying about him. He became completely unfocused and in turn, was unable to do his job properly. Is this starting to sound familiar? One by one, self-sabotaging thoughts began to take hold of his mind. He became so preoccupied with sabotaging himself that his job became jeopardized. His efforts became focused on proving himself in all the wrong ways, in ways that he mistakenly thought would ease his racing mind.

At this point, it might seem hopeless, and you might be wondering what can be done to stop these vicious cycles of self-sabotage. Well, understanding is the first step, and the second step is to learn how to combat them. The best way to get your mind to cooperate with you is to start making small steps towards changing your mindset. The very same process that creates the neurological pathways in your brain that reinforce bad thinking and behavior can also be used to create new, more positive and beneficial pathways in the brain.

In the past, it was believed that your brain developed in childhood and became fixed after this point and that changing the way your brain worked in adulthood wasn't possible. We now know that this isn't true. Our brains are always developing and changing as we adapt to new situations and learn new things. The ability of your brain to continue evolving is known as neuroplasticity, and it allows you to retrain your brain. You are not stuck with the neurological pathways already existing in your brain. You can change your thinking and behaviors and replace them with new patterns of behavior through creating new neural pathways in your brain, that help you achieve what you want out of your life.

In order to take full advantage of neuroplasticity in your brain, you will need to start by uncovering the ways you are sabotaging yourself. You will have to practice introspection and dive into your unconscious mind as much as possible. You will have to take a look at your thinking to understand what exactly you are afraid of, what your stresses are, and you will then need to analyze how this affects your behavior. You will have to take a hard and honest look at yourself and highlight the ways in which you are stopping yourself from going for what you want. Once you have done this, you can start making an effort towards changing your thinking and begin to create new neurological pathways in your mind based on healthier ways of thinking that will have a more lasting positive effect.

This is where positivity comes into play, but instead of throwing a positivity rug over your problems and hoping they go away, you will be dealing with the underlying problems that cause your self-sabotaging thoughts. You will begin to uncover repressed emotions that influence your behavior, and you will be able to, on a neurological level, create positive pathways in your brain that, when made right, will actively affect your behavior in positive ways that will help you. This will prove to be a powerful tool that will make a massive difference in your life, thanks to which you will be effectively stopping your mind from working against you. When practiced and reinforced, this will create new neurological pathways in your brain that will become your new normal behavior. As you begin to stop using the bad pathways that were causing you to sabotage yourself, they will become inactive and will fade away.

If you would like to get professional help in doing this, there are some recommended therapies that would be able to help you on this journey. Talk therapies with a psychoanalytic approach can help you uncover the hidden messages locked away in your subconscious mind, and it can help you gain some perspective on why you behave in certain ways. Therapists allow you to talk about your experiences and revisit your past memories and traumas to help you make links between them and how you think and behave in your everyday life. Therapists who practice psychoanalytic talk therapies use techniques, such as free association, dream therapy, and transference, to help you uncover the hidden messages your subconscious mind is trying to send you.

Free association involves you responding to an image or a word prompt. Based on your responses, the therapist is able to uncover patterns in your thinking that allow them to make observations about what you might be struggling with. Dream therapy relies on you keeping a record of your dreams, and, in much the same way as free association, the therapist will analyze your dreams to uncover recurring patterns and themes that give them insight into your unconscious thoughts. Lastly, transference involves taking a look into your memories from childhood and uncovering your past traumas. This allows the therapist to uncover how you are repeating those traumas in your life and in your relationships in the present day. They are then able to help you move past them by bringing them to your attention and helping you work through them. All of this helps you understand yourself on a deeper level, and it helps you understand your emotions as well as how they affect you.

If you would like help in creating those neurological pathways that aim to eliminate your sabotaging thoughts, then Cognitive Behavioral Therapy (CBT) is a good option for you. Therapists using it focus on uncovering how the way you think affects your emotions and how these two things influence your behavior. CBT proposes that our behavior is a response to our environment, and how we respond is dependent on how we perceive what is happening around us. It involves uncovering what your core beliefs, which you learned in childhood, are. These core beliefs influence your thinking and put in place a rigid set of rules to live by, which can cause you unnecessary problems as you struggle to break out of these ways of thinking. These core beliefs can also lead to self-sabotaging thoughts, such as the ones outlined in this book. Lastly, they observe how this affects your behavior. CBT interventions are aimed at changing your core beliefs and thereby putting a stop to your self-sabotaging thoughts. New, more positive core beliefs can then be put in place to influence behaviors that are more beneficial to you. Much of what is being taught in this book in terms of learning brain hacks to rewire your brain follows the CBT techniques.

Chapter 4: Weapons Against Self-sabotaging

Now we have a firm understanding of what causes us to self-sabotage, of how our brains work to reinforce these kinds of behaviors, and of how we can work to change those behaviors. Thus, it's time to move on to finding new, more positive ways of thinking that can replace your discarded negative ways of thinking. These are the brain hacks you will need to start steering your life in the direction you want. These brain hacks can be used as weapons against self-sabotaging thinking and should be read in relation to chapter 2, where we outlined some of the common self-sabotaging thoughts that we can fall victim to. While they do not directly relate to the sabotaging thoughts discussed, they will go a long way to combat the thinking involved in creating the foundation for those negative thought patterns. There are many more ways in which you can change your thinking and behavior positively. However, listing and discussing them all will take too much of our time together. I have selected a few to discuss here in this chapter, but don't let your research and understanding stop here. Go on to do future research and uncover more weapons against self-sabotage, as this will only help you further your journey to success.

Challenge Your Negative Thoughts

Have you ever realized how sensible you were when you were giving someone else advice, and then wondered to yourself how come you couldn't think sensibly about your own problems? It would probably be the perfect world if we could take our own advice, but that would be a world of emotionless robots. Emotions are what gets in the way of our ability to think rationally, and, unfortunately, the closer you are to a problem and the more personal it is to you, the less likely you are to be able to think rationally. That's why we are unable to take our own advice - our emotions often get in our way. The trick to overcoming this is to take a step outside of yourself for a few moments and think about things more objectively. If you are able to separate yourself in this way, then you will be able to take a look at how you are thinking and feeling in a more rational way.

It's from an objective place that you will be able to gain some perspective on the situation. You will be able to see the flaws in your thinking, and you will be able to see where you are being negative and how this is impacting you. You should then take it a step further and challenge those negative thoughts. Put them under a microscope and inspect if they are valid. More likely than not, you'll begin to see how flawed your negative thought processes are. They will begin to crumble and fall apart, and you will find that getting over them will become a lot less challenging.

This can be much easier to do in theory, and less so in practice. It can be incredibly difficult to separate yourself from your emotions, especially if you are extremely emotionally charged. Gaining perspective when you are angry is particularly difficult. The best advice for these situations is to not act out of anger, but rather to take the time to cool off. Once you've had enough of a cool-down period, you can then try to be more objective about things. You also need to be able to be honest with yourself and recognize that you too have flaws and make mistakes. If you are unwilling to accept this, then you will forever be stuck making those mistakes, rather than moving past them and making the necessary changes to improve yourself.

Shoe on the Other Foot...

Sometimes we get so wrapped up in our own thinking we fail to see things from someone else's perspective. Having more insight into what someone else might be going through can help you develop more compassion and understanding for those around you. This will go a long way in helping you avoid and solve conflicts with the important people in your life. It will also help you develop a real understanding of what others may be thinking. In chapter 2, I mentioned mind reading as being a self-sabotaging pattern of thinking that leads you to falsely think you know what is going on in someone else's head, and this still holds true. Putting yourself in someone else's shoes is different from mind-reading, which involves making assumptions and judgments without any real context or understanding.

When we practice mind-reading, we aren't really viewing things from anyone else's perspective at all. We assume we know what they are thinking from our own limited perspective. A perspective that, more than anything else, highlights our insecurities rather than shedding any real insight into those around us. You reflect your own insecurities back at yourself, as if looking into a mirror. In this way, mind-reading is more a representation of what we think of ourselves and less of what anyone else thinks of us.

When you really make the effort to put yourself in someone else's shoes, you are choosing to view the world as they would. This involves you taking the time to understand them better by getting to know a bit more about them. You would then be able to make more informed assumptions about what their perspective on things is. By doing this, you will be getting out of your own head, you will be gaining a better understanding of the world and the people around you, and you might be surprised at what you will find.

Relinquish Control of Things out of Your Reach

Trying to control everything around us is unhealthy and feeds our anxiety. Realistically, there isn't much we can control in this world other than ourselves and how we react to the situation we find ourselves in. We can't control the people and circumstances around us, and there isn't really any point in trying. When you try to control these situations, you are limiting them and stopping things from playing out naturally as they would if you hadn't interfered. You're also taking on more responsibility for the situation than you need to by assuming that it is up to you to make things run smoothly or go a certain way. This is setting yourself up for failure - because it will never pan out the way you want.

When you try to control the people around you, you will find that you come up against a lot of resistance while people fight you off. This will only leave you frustrated, and it will cause a lot of strain on your relationships. You wouldn't appreciate it if someone else tried to control you, and you shouldn't be surprised when they resist. This has happened to me a few times in social situations where I have found myself being the planner. I decided to plan a dinner with a few friends, and somehow this made me feel responsible for the events of the night. Everyone had to have a good time, and I tried to control the night to ensure that they did. This is a battle I should have known I would lose, because it's not up to me to make sure everyone has a good time, and I'm better off leaving the evening to its own course.

Once you accept this, you begin to feel instant relief, and it can be extremely liberating. The only person you have to really worry about is yourself, and acknowledging this allows you to focus on the things that you can actually control. Namely, the things we are talking about in this book. You can work on mastering your control over your thinking, your emotions, and your behavior.

Counteract the Negative Bias

Since we know that we tend to highlight the negatives in any given situation over the positives, we should take the time to counteract this when at all possible, or when it occurs to us that this is what we are doing. When you find yourself focusing on something negative that happened to you, make yourself stop and take the time to pick out one positive thing that happened to focus on instead. This will help you learn to have more compassion for yourself as you begin to realize that you are being too hard on yourself by always focusing on what you are doing wrong or on how things are going wrong. You will also begin to see the things you do right more easily as time goes on, and it will become easier for you to enjoy your accomplishments.

You could also make this a daily habit by practicing it regularly. Find a time in your day to dedicate to thinking about something good that happened that day or something good that you accomplished and can be proud of. You could, for example, do this when you're lying in bed before you fall asleep and you're thinking about the events of your day. Make a concerted effort to play back a positive event that happened, and really take the time to relive it through all of your five senses. This will ensure that the positive memory will be committed to your long-term memory more strongly than the negative events of your day will be. You are more likely to reinforce new behaviors and thought patterns if they are associated with positive memories. It will also go a long way in counteracting the negative bias that we so easily fall victim to.

Minimize Your Expectations

By having expectations in life, you are choosing to live in the future rather than focusing on the present. Foresight is a valuable skill to have, and it allows you to anticipate possible challenges that you may come across, which allows you to make choices to avoid them ahead of time. You could be expecting it to rain that day, and so you take an umbrella with you before you leave the house, saving yourself from being drenched on your way to work. You know you've gone too far in investing too much in your expectations when they become unrealistic or when you start to invest too much into them. You'll begin to feel put out when things don't happen as you anticipated, or when you feel let down by someone because they didn't do exactly what you wanted or needed.

Having expectations is not a substitute for communication, and if you want something you'd be better off being upfront about it. It is also worth accepting that it's no one's responsibility to meet your expectations just because you have them. They aren't the ones who created them, and it's unfair of you to place that responsibility on them. No one is going to be as invested in what you want or think as you are, because everybody has their own lives to focus on and worry about. That's not to say that there aren't going to be people around you that love and care for you. There are, of course, and they will be there to offer support and advice when needed, but they aren't there to fix your life for you. That's all up to you.

Having unrealistic expectations can also cause you unnecessary anxiety and stress, as you worry about future events that you have no real way of knowing will happen or not. When you minimize your expectations and instead take things as they come, you are able to save yourself all the worry and spend your time and focus on dealing with challenges as they arise. You also learn to be more communicative about what you're thinking and feeling, and about what you want out of your relationship or the situations you find yourself in.

Set Solid Goals and Plans

You may think that, due to the self-sabotaging thought processes behind creating unrealistic expectations, planning for the future is a bad idea. However, this is not the case. If you recognize when you are pinning your hopes and happiness on future events, then you will know you are heading into dangerous territory. As long as you avoid doing this, planning for the future can be a useful tool that will help you reach your goals. We tend not to plan for the future because we believe that this will rob us of our flexibility to change our goals as we go. We also want to remain adaptable in case we don't end up reaching our goals. However, planning won't take your flexibility or adaptability away. If your plan doesn't work out the way you hoped it would, then you get to work restructuring your plan to adapt to your new circumstances.

You will need to begin by setting yourself solid goals. Once you have these, you can begin to set out your plan on how to achieve them. These plans will form the road map that will set you up on a structured path that will ensure you don't lose momentum or lose your way. Make you fully understand what it is that you hope to achieve and why you are working towards it. Don't, for example, set goals for yourself for the wrong reasons. Be sure that what you are planning to work towards is something you want to achieve - for yourself and your happiness. If you get stuck in your planning, perhaps you can't clearly see all the steps in how you are going to achieve your goals. You may find it useful to try reverse engineering your goals and plans to achieve them. This will help you see the steps from a new perspective that may shed some light on the steps needed in your planning.

You can also look for role models and mentorships in order to find out what steps they took to get to where they are. After all, everyone needs some help and advice along the way. Nobody gets to where they are alone in this world. Another thing to note is that when you set your goals, do so while keeping your limits in mind. Don't set yourself up for failure by setting large, unrealistic goals that put you under unnecessary pressure. This will only overwhelm you, and when you inevitably fail to carry out the steps necessary to reach your goal, you will begin to feel demotivated and like you are unable to accomplish anything. Rather, set yourself smaller realistic goals, with solid plans on how to get there. Over time, these smaller goals will turn into that larger goal you hope to achieve. Each milestone you meet will also lead to you building up your confidence and your ability to handle your success. Take the time to appreciate what you have accomplished each time you meet a milestone, don't undermine your successes. Enjoy what you have accomplished and allow yourself to feel proud.

Practice Makes Perfect

To rewire your brain and create new neurological pathways for thinking and behavior that allow you to stop sabotaging yourself, you need to practice repetition. The whole concept behind creating new pathways in your brain relies on you repeating the new patterns of thinking and behaving. This will ensure that the old pathways dedicated to your self-sabotaging ways will become unused and inactive. The brain is like a muscle that needs to be trained and exercised regularly. This can prove to be difficult, especially if you keep finding yourself falling back into old habits and becoming demotivated about keeping it up. Even when we have the best intentions to improve ourselves and change our lives, whether physically or mentally, we can still find it to be an impossible task as life continuously gets in the way.

Try to remember that even the smallest changes will begin to make a difference in your life, and that reading this book has already gone a long way in helping you achieve this. You have taken the time to understand yourself better, don't minimize your efforts. The key is not to finish reading this book and expect everything to change overnight. Change takes time and effort, and it may take a few failed attempts before anything sticks. If you find yourself reverting back to self-sabotaging, just brush yourself off and start again. Find ways to create new routines in your day that will help you practice your new ways of thinking and behaving more easily. These will be tailored to your own subjective needs, as they will be dependent on the kinds of self-sabotaging thoughts and behaviors you exhibit. They will also be heavily determined by your lifestyle and daily routines. So, do research and find out what other people do to find small ways to change their lives, and get creative with how you find ways to change yours.

Chapter 5: A Healthier Lifestyle for a Healthier Mind

Researchers and healthcare professionals have become increasingly focused on and aware of how important it is to have a healthy mental state and how this affects your overall well-being. Gone are the days where we focus solely on physical health, and shy away from the taboo topic of mental illness and discussing your feelings. We now know that physical health and mental health are two parts of a whole that are integrated with one another and influence each other in ways we are still yet to understand. If we are going to use the tools and knowledge that this book teaches, it would be wise to use every advantage available to you to help you make the changes you need to make in your life.

Having an overall healthy well-being is definitely an advantage we could all use. Not only will this improve your physical health and help you fight off illness and fatigue, it will also help you gain mental strength and focus. Having good mental health means you will be better equipped to deal with and overcome the challenges life throws your way. The best way to promote your overall well-being is to find ways in which you can improve your lifestyle. Take the time to take inventory of your life, make a note of the ways in which you live an unhealthy lifestyle and work at finding better ways to live that will promote health. Here are two suggestions that I have found to be quite beneficial for anyone wanting to improve their lives in this way. The first is to practice mindfulness to help improve your mental health, and the second is to exercise and change your diet and eat healthier food that improves brain functioning and mood. This will not only improve your physical health but your mental health as well.

What Is Mindfulness?

Mindfulness is by no means a new mental health movement, it dates back hundreds of years, having its roots in Eastern culture. However, is has been increasingly popular in Western culture in the past decade. It is a way of living that involves being more present in the moment and treating yourself with more kindness, compassion, and understanding. It has proven to have some positive effects on improving focus and concentration, and it goes a long way in helping to reduce stress, anxiety, and depression. It's a method that has proven to be successful in helping regulate your emotions, rather than being ruled by them, and it has also proven to help to gain a better understanding of and control over your emotions.

Have you ever gotten in your car and started driving, listening to the radio playing in the background as you make your way through traffic, but when you get to your destination, you park your can and as you turn off the engine you suddenly think, "Did I drive here?". You were so unmindful of what was happening around you that you didn't even remember driving there, you simply did it on autopilot, missing the entire journey. This is how a lot of us live our lives on a daily basis. We clock out of our own minds and go on with the motions, not paying attention to anything and not taking anything in. This causes us to miss out on a lot of our lives. We miss important information about things and situations going on around us. Insights into ourselves, our emotions, and our relationships. Mindfulness teaches you how to be present in the moment in a certain way, and it teaches you to be more aware of yourself and your environment in a way that can help you pay more attention to the things that you can learn from and that can help you improve yourself. It teaches you to view yourself, your thoughts, your emotions, and the world around you with calmness and compassion.

As mentioned previously in this book in relation to overgeneralizing, a lot of people also allow their thoughts and emotions in the present moment to become affected by possible future events. We also tend to allow this to happen due to past events and traumas that we haven't quite managed to overcome. These past traumas can cause you to act out in the present moment in ways that make situations worse, or it can lead to repeated cycles of behavior that we get stuck in because we are unable to move past them. This is commonly seen in toxic relationships, where a person keeps finding themselves in relationships with people who leave them heartbroken time and time again.

We do this because we are living mindlessly, and it hasn't occurred to us that there is a better way. Mindfulness teaches you to not focus so much on your past or on the future. It teaches you how to be aware of what you are thinking, of your emotions, and of what is going on around you in a more constructive and objective way. This allows you to dispel negative emotions more easily rather than act on them. You are then able to act in a more informed way that helps you rather than harms you. The practices of mindfulness falls in line with some of the positive counteractive thinking spoken about in chapter 4, and using mindfulness techniques alongside changing your thinking in this way will help you reinforce the changes you need to make in order to change your mindset.

Mindfulness techniques go a long way in helping you rewire your brain, and they can be used alongside the tools taught in this book to help you create positive thoughts and behaviors. When we allow ourselves to be overcome by our emotions, then we are opening ourselves up to behaving in reactive ways. People who are quick to anger or people who are prone to anxiety are allowing their emotions to take over. Their immediate response to these emotions is to act on them. Someone who gets angry will find themselves snapping at people around them, and someone who gets anxiety will find themselves avoiding situations that exacerbate their anxiety. All of these situations condition the brain, these thoughts linked to these behaviors repeated over and over create those neural pathways in your brain that you're trying to stop. Mindfulness is an intervention tool that will prevent those reactions by helping you regulate your emotions and avoid acting on them. This will help you render those neural pathways leading to your sabotaging behaviors useless.

How to Be More Mindful

Mindfulness coaches teach methods such as mindfulness meditation, where you focus on your breathing and your senses to calm your mind and be present. It has been shown to improve brain cognition, it reduces stress, anxiety and fatigue, and it improves spatial awareness and memory. It allows you to gain mastery and focus over your mind. There is also mindfulness-based cognitive therapy, which combines mindfulness techniques with cognitive behavioral therapy, which goes a long way in helping you change bad habits and behaviors in order to create those new neurological pathways in your brain. Other mindfulness activities that are helpful include yoga and body awareness. These are both activities that also focus on bringing your attention to your body or breathing in order to bring you into the present moment.

However, you don't need to rely on mindfulness coaches in yoga classes to bring more mindfulness into your life. You can practice mindfulness in your daily life all on your own. Here are some tips on how and when you can be more mindful every day. Whenever you start a new task, take a few moments to concentrate on your breathing and calm yourself. Reign in your thoughts and focus your attention on the present moment. This can be done before you go to a meeting, in your car before you go about your day, or over a cup of coffee before you start work. Your method for counteracting the negative bias before you go to bed, where you focus on a positive event in your day, is another way of being mindful, and you can practice these two in conjunction with one another.

Practice mindfulness in the middle of an ongoing situation. If you find yourself in the middle of a conflict or you begin to feel overwhelmed by your emotions, stop and take a deep breath, and bring yourself back into the present moment. Focus on your breathing to regain control of your emotions and focus within your mind. This will prevent you from acting out rashly, which will cause you to worsen the situation or conflict you find yourself in. You don't need to wait for a high-stress situation to do this, you can also do it when you're doing a mindless physical activity, like washing the dishes or watering your plants. Through this, you will learn to enjoy the simpler pleasures in life and this will add some much-needed calmness and serenity to your day.

You can also practice mindfulness whenever you find yourself in the quiet moments of your life, standing idly in line at the grocery store, or waiting around for someone to come and meet up with you, or in the shopping queue. Bring yourself into the present moment, focus on your breathing, and try to take in everything that is going on around you. Experience the world through all of your five senses and be pleasantly surprised at how much more you begin to notice about what is going on both inside your own mind and around you. You will also begin to notice how much you have been missing out on in your life. You might notice how beautiful the sky looks or how you enjoy watching the people around you go about their lives.

Sometimes you might notice things that come up that are

hurtful and that you don't want to look at emotionally. You will be tempted to push those hurtful thoughts and feelings away, but mindfulness urges you not to. It teaches you that you should try to accept your emotions, positive or negative, and try to understand them through a lense of calm, kindness and compassion towards yourself. Instead of being hard on yourself or allowing those emotions to overtake you, you deal with them in a more meaningful way that has proven to have positive effects on the lives of those practicing it.

Mental Health and a Healthy Diet

It has been known for a long time that a healthy diet is necessary for your overall physical health. Eating healthily ensures that you maintain a healthy body weight, it keeps your heart healthy and it builds up your immune system to help fight off germs and infections that could make you ill. However, more recently, mental health professionals are becoming increasingly aware of how diet can also have an impact on your mental health. In fact, it is becoming more and more apparent that food can have as much of an impact on your mental health as it does on your physical health. This has opened up a whole new field of study and research known as nutritional psychiatry. Researchers have found that an unhealthy diet consisting of high fat, high carbohydrate foods can lead to poor mental functioning, low moods and it could even be a contributing factor to causing higher levels of stress, depression, and anxiety.

One study in particular provided results that showed that an unhealthy diet increased the risk of depression by 80% in subjects participating in the research. One the other hand, studies have been conducted to show that a healthy diet can have a significant positive effect on your overall mental well-being and can reduce feelings of depression and anxiety. Healthy eating is in no way a substitute for medications and other treatments directed at bettering mental health. However, mental health professionals are beginning to realize the added benefits of including a healthy diet in intervention plans when treating patients with mental illness. While further study needs to be done on the link between diet and mental health to better understand how diet affects brain function and mood, what is already known is proving to be vital knowledge in helping improve your mental well-being. Having good mental health and brain functioning will help you in your pursuit to gain focus and mastery over your brain in the way that this book is trying to teach you to do.

Athletes take the time to look after themselves mentally and physically to allow their bodies to perform as well as possible. We should all take a page out of their book and do all that we can to help our brains reach their full potential.

Ways in Which Healthy Eating Improves Mental Health

When you eat healthy food, you're promoting the growth of

much needed healthy gut bacteria. This good bacteria has a dual positive effect on boosting your overall mental health. It helps to fight bad germs in your body and strengthens your immune system. On a physiological level, having a healthy immune system prevents you from getting ill, keeping your body healthy. Having a weak immune system leads to illness, and being ill can lead to a low mood and feelings of depression as your body struggles to fight off the infection. You're forced to stay indoors, bedridden, and isolated from others. Isolation and loneliness have been known to cause low mood and depression. This all has a negative effect on your overall mental health.

A healthy immune system is your body's best way of fending off illnesses and preventing this from happening, and eating healthy is a sure way of boosting your immune system. Having healthy bacteria in your body also has a direct positive effect on the functioning of your brain by helping the creation of vitamin B. This vitamin helps to promote the production of neurotransmitters, which are the essential chemicals in the brain that help neurons send messages to one another. This will help prevent dementia and strengthen memory. It will also help you in your work of rewiring your brain.

Vitamin B aside, an overall healthy diet will help improve your brain's functioning and neuroplasticity by promoting the transmission of neural signals from cells and neurons in the brain. You need healthy, high-in-nutrients food to feed your brain the protein and enzymes it needs to promote the activity from neuron to neuron and from your brain to the rest of your body. This will help you develop and reinforce the neural pathways that will begin to change your behavior and stop your self-sabotaging thinking. It will also make your thinking sharper, improve your memory, and help prevent you from feeling sluggish or experiencing brain fog.

A Diet for Better Mental Health

Avoid eating foods that are high in calories and low in nutrients, such as processed foods and foods high in unhealthy fats and sugar. Instead, eat food that are packed full of nutrients, such as fresh fruits and vegetables, whole grains, and healthy fats. This diet is the ideal one for a healthier brain and it will promote a much better overall mental health. Eat foods that are high in Omega-3 fatty acids, folic acids, vitamins D and B, magnesium, zinc, and iron. Omega-3s improve thinking and memory. Low levels of zinc have been shown to lead to depression, whereas high levels of zinc help your body fight off stress. Low levels of iron have also been known to lead to low mood and depression.

Mental Health and Exercise

Regular exercise has proven to have many advantages and benefits for your overall physical and mental health. It helps reduce levels of stress and anxiety, and it also helps with lifting your mood by increasing endorphins and chemicals in your brain such as serotonin. It raises your blood pressure and pumps more blood and oxygen to your brain, which improves brain function. It removes brain fog which slows down your thinking and inhibits your brain's ability to retain memories. Brain scanning technology has also been able to prove that exercising regularly also increases the volume of activity in areas of the brain associated with memory and learning, areas such as the hippocampus, the prefrontal cortex, and the medial cortex.

Exercise also boosts your self-esteem by helping you get into shape. It makes you feel strong and capable, which builds your confidence and makes you feel good about yourself. It also allows for more social interaction, since many forms of exercise involve a sport or you joining a class or a gym. This gets you out there into the world and out of your comfort zone, experiencing new things and meeting new people. This helps eliminate feelings of loneliness, and it stops you from isolating yourself from the world, which can only exacerbate your feelings of depression and anxiety.

What Exercise Is Good for the Brain?

Any activity that involves cardiovascular exercise is good for brain functioning and mental health. This increases your heart rate, breathing and blood pressure, which causes an increase of blood and oxygen to the brain. You should be doing about 1 hour of moderate-intensity exercise at least twice a week. You could do an hour of brisk walking or running twice a week and that will be enough to start seeing improvements in your brain functioning. However, we all struggle to stay motivated to be healthy, and it is important to find ways to make exercising fun and easily accessible. Perhaps join a team by taking up a sport, or maybe meet up with a friend on a regular basis and play tennis or squash. If walking or running isn't your thing you can always try swimming or dancing.

Chapter 6: What Is Success Anyway?

We all have our own lives to live, and no one's journey will be the same as anyone else's. Since your life is completely unique to you, there isn't really any point in looking at the lives of others and making comparisons with your own. You should have your own subjective ideas about what you want to achieve in your life, and you should be working towards your goals in your own time and on your own terms. Be confident in who you are, what you want, and what you are trying to accomplish. This also relates to your success. There is no right way to be successful. They may say that "beauty is in the eye of the beholder," and you could say that success is in the eye of those striving towards it. Your success is whatever you want it to be, big or small, it's all relative. If your lifelong dream is to become the President, then that's great. Go for it, and good luck to you because you probably have one hell of a journey ahead of you. If your dream is to become the world's fastest blanket crocheter, then that's great too. No dream is less important than anyone else's. As long as you're happy and being productive in your life, you're on the right path, so carry on, and don't stop yourself from going for those dreams because you get stuck comparing your dreams to ones that seem bigger than yours.

Remember Catherine, the free-spirited traveler who was still trying to figure herself and her life out? The reason she began to feel so lost and hopeless was because she began to feel as if she hadn't achieved as much in her life as her friends had. She started to compare her life to those around her, and somehow, she had decided that her achievements didn't measure up against the achievements of those around her. However, her thinking was flawed because she missed out on a vital point. The success of those around her was never the kind of thing she had ever wanted. What made her friends happy wouldn't necessarily have made her happy if she was in their place. She lost sight of what she wanted, and her perceptions of what would make her feel happy and successful became warped. She also forgot about what she had in her life to be proud of, she had discarded her own achievements.

However, she began to realize this on her own. She remembered what it was that actually made her happy, and that was to travel. She then remembered why she had made the decision to go and travel in the first place, and she recognized that she wouldn't want to go back and change it. She would pack her bags and go without a second thought. It took her realizing this for her to eventually pull herself out of her rut and overcome her depression. She remembered who she was, and she stopped comparing herself, her life, and her achievements against others and accepted that her journey was her own. This brought her peace, and she was then able to focus her mind on figuring out what she wanted and going for it. She went on to travel for another couple of years before eventually getting a job writing about her many travels.

If you'd like to do the same and find happiness and success in your life, then you will need to do as Catherine did. You will need to stop comparing yourself to others and figure out what it is that you want out of your life. Once you figure that out, then you will be able to focus your mind and go for it.

Failure, Friend or Foe?

For a lot of us, failure isn't an option, and it's something we avoid at all costs. We are afraid to fail and so we don't take risks and we don't try new things. We are trying to avoid the feelings of disappointment, embarrassment, depression, and worthlessness that we think we will experience if we do not succeed. In our minds, if we fail, then we ourselves are failures. Does this kind of thinking sound familiar? It's black and white thinking, and it causes people to be too overly critical and hard on themselves. It stops people from ever trying new things, and it keeps them in their comfort zones. This is unfortunate because when you don't go out into the world and try new things, you're locking yourself away and limiting yourself from all that you could experience, from what you could learn, and from what you could go on to accomplish had you just tried.

You may try to tell yourself that this doesn't bother you, but deep down it will and you will be left wondering what if you had tried. Many people never overcome their fear of failure because the more they avoid it, the more they learn to fear it. Eventually, the fear of failure becomes greater than the failure itself. However, it's a mistake to think this way, because contrary to your instinct to avoid it, failure is not a bad thing. It's a necessary part of life and it's good for you to experience. In fact, if you aren't experiencing any failure, then you're doing something wrong. People who fail are people who are trying, and in the long run, this will work out better for them. These people are taking more risks and experiencing more things in life, and they are learning to overcome their fear of failure. This builds their resilience to it and makes them stronger.

I've always disliked the saying, "The grass isn't always greener on the other side." It always left me baffled because I would think to myself, "...but it could be." I could just pop over and see, and if it wasn't greener, then I'll just pop right back. However, it doesn't work like that. The saying is meant as a warning and as a cautionary tale for all who dare to venture out of their comfort zone. I didn't want to get caught up in this catch 22, and in the end, curiosity won me over. I decided that I would rather try new things and see for myself which grass I liked best, greener or not, and if I didn't like what I found... Well then, I'd just find some greener grass elsewhere. Failing will teach you this because it's better to have tried than to have not tried at all. It is through our failures that we learn what it is that we really want in life, and it's from these experiences that we find the drive and determination to pick ourselves up and try again.

Imagine you have a dream to be a brilliant dancer that performs on stage for hundreds of people. So, you go for a dance lesson to help you on your way of fulfilling this dream. Much to your horror, you realize you have no rhythm whatsoever, and you completely embarrass yourself in front of the class and your teacher. You feel like a failure, and your dreams of becoming a dancer begin to crumble before your eyes. At this point, you have two choices. The first is to give up, but be satisfied that although failed, you still tried and you will never have to wonder if you could have made your dreams of becoming a dancer a reality. Through this experience, you have learned that maybe it wasn't your dream after all, and you learned that you can overcome failure. You can now move on to try something new that could open up a whole new door of possibilities for you.

The second choice you could make is to decide that even though you have no rhythm, you love to dance and you're not ready to admit defeat and give up on your dream to become that dancer you know you can be. So, you keep at it and you go to dance class after dance class because you are determined to put in the hard work necessary to improve your abilities. You find this determination because through your failure, you realized that this dream is important to you and that it is worth working for.

Conclusion

In reading this book, you have gone on a journey to better understand your mind. You have begun to develop an understanding of the complexity of human psychology. We have learned about the unconscious mind and about the negative and anxious thoughts that live there. These thoughts push through into our conscious mind and influence our behavior in ways that, if we don't pay attention to them, could be quite harmful to our mental well-being. This can lead to you unintentionally sabotage your own life and stop yourself from achieving happiness and success. I have highlighted some of the ways in which we practice self-sabotaging thoughts, and we have begun to uncover how they can influence your behavior and how they can cause problems in your life. This pattern of thinking and behaving becomes wired into our brain and we carry it out in our daily lives completely automatically and unconsciously. This is why it is important to learn ways in which you can begin to combat these negative thoughts and break this repeating cycle in your life.

Thankfully, our brains are amazing organs that are easily adaptable and can continue to grow throughout our lives due to their neuroplasticity. By training our brains to think differently, we can create new patterns of thinking and behaving that can put an end to our self-sabotaging ways. When practiced and repeated, these new patterns become the new normal and our brains will begin to think and behave in this way automatically and naturally. This will ensure that we are able to stop holding ourselves back and finally work towards our happiness and success.

I also outlined some of the ways in which you can change your thinking to be more positive and beneficial in your life. These ways of thinking challenge your self-sabotaging thoughts and offer you a new perspective on things. There are, of course, ways in which you can help this process, and we discussed a few of them. You can seek professional help, which will speed up your ability to rewire your brain and ensure that you are learning more about the ways in which you can improve your mental health and your thinking. You can change your lifestyle and lead a healthier life through healthy eating and exercise that will strengthen your body and mind. This will ensure that you have every advantage to better yourself and your mental well-being. You can also practice mindfulness in your everyday life to help you manage your often overwhelming emotions. This will help you find some much needed calm and patience in your life, not only for yourself but for your environment and for the people in your life as well.

While this is a lot to take in, and it will take a lot of effort to implement all the things that you have learned through reading this book, it's important to know that any change worth having takes time. You are going to have to continuously work on yourself as life takes you through many twists and turns. However if you have really taken in what you have learned through reading this book, then you will realize that the tools taught here are not only meant to help you stop your self-sabotaging thoughts, they're also aimed at helping you develop and grow yourself in a way that will enable you to deal with any challenges life sends your way. It takes a holistic view of the human condition, to better understand it and find ways in which we can strive to be better.

Thank you for reading my book, I would be very grateful if you could leave a review.

References

Fitzgerald, D. (2011). Nutrition and Mental Health. Retrieved from https://familydoctor.org/nutrition-mental-health/

Diet and mental health. (2015). Retrieved from https://www.mentalhealth.org.uk/a-to-z/d/diet-and-mental-health

Miller, K. (2019). Can What You Eat Affect Your Mental Health?. Retrieved from https://www.webmd.com/mental-health/news/20150820/food-mental-health#4

Godman, H. (2014). Regular exercise changes the brain to improve memory, thinking skills - Harvard Health Blog. Retrieved from https://www.health.harvard.edu/blog/regular-exercise-changes-brain-improve-memory-thinking-skills-201404097110

Exercise and mental health. (2019). Retrieved from https://www.healthdirect.gov.au/exercise-and-mental-health

6 Scientifically Proven Benefits Of Mindfulness And Meditation. (2019). Retrieved from https://www.forbes.com/sites/jeenacho/2016/07/14/10-scientifically-proven-benefits-of-mindfulness-and-meditation/#7f1d9bf063ce

How Do I Bring More Mindfulness Into My Life? - Mindful. (2019). Retrieved from https://www.mindful.org/how-do-i-bring-more-mindfulness-into-my-life/

Julia Kristina Counselling. (2017). What is Mindfulness? And How Does it Help Decrease Anxiety? [YouTube]. Retrieved from https://www.youtube.com/watch?v=4zDSF9pTVOc

The Neuroscience of Behavior Change. (2017). Retrieved from https://healthtransformer.co/the-neuroscience-of-behavior-change-bcb567fa83c1

Julia Kristina Counselling. (2018). What Is Self-Sabotage & How To Know If You're Doing It [YouTube]. Retrieved from https://www.youtube.com/watch?v=CIW5qVInlQE

Julia Kristina Counselling. (2019). 5 Ways You're Subconsciously Sabotaging Yourself [YouTube]. Retrieved from https://www.youtube.com/watch?v=GCu7Isn6geM

Wilding, M. (n.d.). 5 Different Types of Imposter Syndrome (and 5 Ways to Battle Each One). Retrieved from https://www.themuse.com/advice/5-different-types-of-imposter-syndrome-and-5-ways-to-battle-each-one

Gattuso, R. (2018, July 31). 5 Ways Black and White Thinking Poisons Your Perspective. Retrieved from https://www.talkspace.com/blog/black-white-thinking-ways-poisons-your-perspective/

Paul, A. M. (2007, September). Mind Reading. Retrieved from https://www.psychologytoday.com/us/articles/200709/mind-reading

Cuncic, A. (2019, November 18). Overgeneralization and Social Anxiety. Retrieved from https://www.verywellmind.com/overgeneralization-3024614

Cherry, K. (2019, July 26). What Is the Negativity Bias? Retrieved from https://www.verywellmind.com/negative-bias-4589618

Johnson, J.A. (2018, February 17). The Psychology of Expectations. Retrieved from https://www.psychologytoday.com/gb/blog/cui-bono/201802/the-psychology-expectations

How the Conscious Mind Was Studied by Freud. (2019). Retrieved from https://www.verywellmind.com/what-is-the-conscious-mind-2794984

The Structure and Levels of the Mind According to Freud. (2019). Retrieved from https://www.verywellmind.com/the-conscious-and-unconscious-mind-2795946

What Is the Unconscious (and Why Is It Like an Iceberg)?.

(2019). Retrieved from https://www.verywellmind.com/what-is-the-unconscious-2796004

10 Common Negative Thinking Patterns and How You Can Change Them - The Best Brain Possible. (2018). Retrieved from https://thebestbrainpossible.com/negative-thinking-depression-mind/

Cicetti, F. (2013). Can Negative Thoughts Be Stopped?. Retrieved from https://www.livescience.com/36586-stop-negative-thoughts-depression.html

Social Comparison Theory | Psychology Today UK. (2019). Retrieved 25 November 2019, from https://www.psychologytoday.com/gb/basics/social-comparison-theory

Social Development Theory. (2014). Retrieved from https://www.learning-theories.com/vygotskys-social-learning-theory.html

Social Learning Theory Bandura Social Learning Theory. (2019). Retrieved from https://www.learning-theories.com/social-learning-theory-bandura.html

7 Ways to Deal With Negative Thoughts. (2019). Retrieved from https://www.psychologytoday.com/gb/blog/women-s-mental-health-matters/201509/7-ways-deal-negative-thoughts

Hughes, L. (2019). How to Stop Feeling Anxious Right Now. Retrieved from https://www.webmd.com/mental-health/features/ways-to-reduce-anxiety

Gozenonline. (2012). Anxiety: Why Humans Experience Anxiety [YouTube]. Retrieved from https://www.youtube.com/watch?v=7W_rlrwH-BE

Patel, D. (2018). 8 Ways to Stop Self-Sabotaging Your Success. Retrieved from https://www.entrepreneur.com/article/324900

Self-Sabotage | Psychology Today UK. (2019). Retrieved from https://www.psychologytoday.com/gb/basics/self-sabotage

Adam Sicinski. (n.d.). Do you Sabotage your Own Success? Here's How to Stop Self-Sabotage in its Tracks! Retrieved from https://blog.iqmatrix.com/overcome-self-sabotage

The Top 3 Reasons Why You Self-Sabotage and How to Stop. (2019). Retrieved from https://www.psychologytoday.com/gb/blog/the-mindful-self-express/201806/the-top-3-reasons-why-you-self-sabotage-and-how-stop

The School of Life. (2016). The Impostor Syndrome [YouTube]. Retrieved from https://www.youtube.com/watch?v=eqhUHyVpAwE

Magical Thinking. (2019). Retrieved from https://www.psychologytoday.com/gb/blog/happiness-in-world/200911/magical-thinking

Sentis. (2012). Neuroplasticity [YouTube] Retrieved from https://www.youtube.com/watch?v=ELpfYCZa87g

Julia Kristina Counselling. (2017). How To Get Past Your Fear of Failure [YouTube]. Retrieved from https://www.youtube.com/watch?v=A4Hf_LuRjU

Byrne, M. & Fenn, K. (2019). The key principles of cognitive behavioural therapy. InnovAiT, 6(9), 579–585. doi/pdf/10.1177/1755738012471029

Psychoanalytic Therapy | Psychology Today UK. (2019). Retrieved 25 November 2019, from https://www.psychologytoday.com/gb/therapy-types/psychoanalytic-therapy

History of Mindfulness: From East to West and Religion to Science. (2017). Retrieved from https://positivepsychology.com/history-of-mindfulness/

Julia Kristina Counselling. (2018). Quick Stress & Anxiety Reduction - Mindfulness Exercise (No Meditation Required!) [YouTube]. Retrieved from https://www.youtube.com/watch?v=hKtKQ_AGxYg

B is for Brain Health - Healthy Brains by Cleveland Clinic. (2017). Retrieved from https://healthybrains.org/b-brain-health/

Mcleod, S. (2019). Stress, Illness and the Immune System | Simply Psychology. Retrieved 27 November 2019, from https://www.simplypsychology.org/stress-immune.html

Psychoanalytic Therapy | Psychology Today UK. (2019). Retrieved from https://www.psychologytoday.com/gb/therapy-types/psychoanalytic-therapy

Sicinski, A. (2016). The Ultimate Guide for Saying "NO" When it Matters Most!. Retrieved from https://blog.iqmatrix.com/saying-no

Sicinski, A. (2013). How to Develop a Solid Plan of Action for Goal Achievement. Retrieved 27 November 2019, from https://blog.iqmatrix.com/plan-of-action

The Psychology of Lateness. (2019). Retrieved from https://welldoing.org/article/lateness